Commissioned by the American Guild of Organists's
1999 Region IV Convention (Knoxville Chapter)

Sonata da chiesa (1998)

for flute and organ

by

Dan Locklair

ISBN 0-634-00909-5

RICORDI

DISTRIBUTED BY

7777 W. BLUEMOUND RD. P.O. BOX 13819 MILWAUKEE, WI 53213

Sonata da chiesa (1998)
for flute and organ
by
Dan Locklair

Commissioned by the American Guild of Organists's 1999 Regional Convention (Knoxville, Tennessee Chapter), my **Sonata da chiesa (1998)** is written for flute and a one-manual, three-stop (8',4',2') portative organ with short keyboard (C – F) and no pedal. Approximately twelve minutes in length, **Sonata da chiesa (1998)** is easily adaptable to a larger organ by following the spirit of the registration suggestions given throughout the piece.

Historically, the terms *sonata da chiesa* (church sonata) and *sonata da camera* (chamber sonata) had their roots in the early baroque period (early 1600's) and referred not to a form or genre but to a place of performance (church or court respectively). Later, the Italian composer, Archangelo Corelli (1653-1713), standardized the *sonata da chiesa* as a four-movement piece with a slow-fast-slow-fast tempo scheme and the *sonata da camera* as a suite of several traditional binary form dance movements, usually preceded by an introduction.

My **Sonata da chiesa (1998),** composed during the late spring and early summer of 1998, is influenced by the spirit of the baroque and by a number of qualities inherent in the *sonata da chiesa* and the *sonata da camera*. In many ways, the sacred and secular are bridged in **Sonata da chiesa (1998)**.

As with the traditional *sonata da chiesa,* **Sonata da chiesa (1998)** follows a slow-fast-slow-fast four-movement scheme. Not typical of the traditional *sonata da chiesa*, yet reflecting the influence of the church, is the well-known 16th century chorale melody, *Wie schön leuchtet* ("How Brightly Shines the Morning Star") which forms the melodic basis for the first and third movements (as well as the AAB form of **Movement 1**). Attributed to Philipp Nicolai (1556-1608), this melody has long been one of Germany's most popular chorale melodies, as it is particularly associated with weddings and other church festival occasions.

The most obvious *sonata da camera* quality of **Sonata da chiesa (1998)** is the place of its World Premiere : The Knoxville Museum of Art (28 June 1999, André Lash, organist). All four movements, in some way, display the spirit of dance, but there are no traditional baroque dances present. **Movement 4** is the only movement that is in the traditional two-part, binary form of dances making up baroque suites, although **Movement 1** is influenced by the baroque dance, the *sarabande*. Though not a dance form, the baroque ground bass technique, *chaconne*, is at the heart of **Movement 3** and this *chaconne* is previewed in both **Movements 1** and **2**. In the baroque *sonata da camera,* as in all baroque suites, all the pieces are in the same key. In **Sonata da chiesa (1998)** each of the four movements is based on the same tonal center, C (**1** : C Major; **2** : C Lydian mode; **3** : C chromatic; **4** : I /IV C major/F major "Amen cadence" chords, alternating with the same I/IV harmonies of E major/A major).

Subtitles are given for each movement, which provide the extra-musical stimuli. These subtitles are similar to those found in topical indices of hymnals and here help frame the piece. While it is best for the composition to be played as a whole, individual movements may be excerpted.

I wish to express my thanks to the Knoxville AGO Region IV Convention Committee for offering me this commission.

Duration :
1. **Processional - "Beginning of Worship"** : ca. 2' 10"
2. **"Adoration and Praise"** : ca. 2' 30"
3. **"Faith and Aspiration" (Chaconne)** : ca. 4' 20"
4. **Amen - "Close of Worship"** : ca. 3
Total duration : ca. 12 minutes

Dan Locklair
Winston-Salem, North Carolina (USA), Summer 1998

*Commissioned by the American Guild of Organists's
1999 Region IV Convention (Knoxville Chapter)*

Sonata da chiesa (1998)
for flute and organ

1. Processional - "Beginning of Worship"

Dan Locklair

Moderate and stately tempo (♩ = ca. 88)

*This piece is conceived for a one-manual organ of three stops (8', 4', 2')
with limited manual compass and no pedal division. Dynamics given in the organ part are
approximations : *mp*= 8'; *mf*=8',4', *f*=8',4',2'

Slowing - **In tempo**

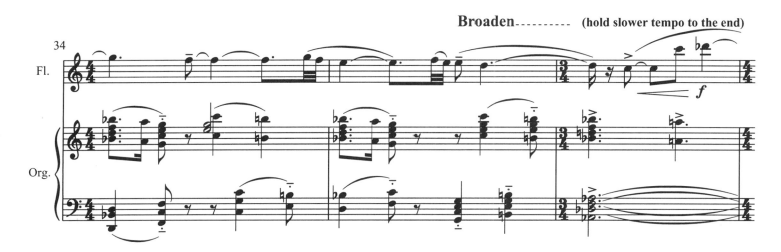

2. "Adoration and Praise"

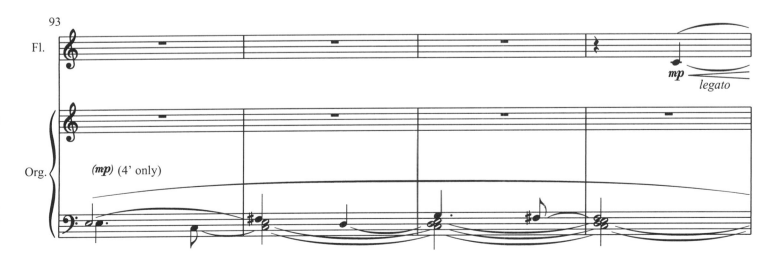

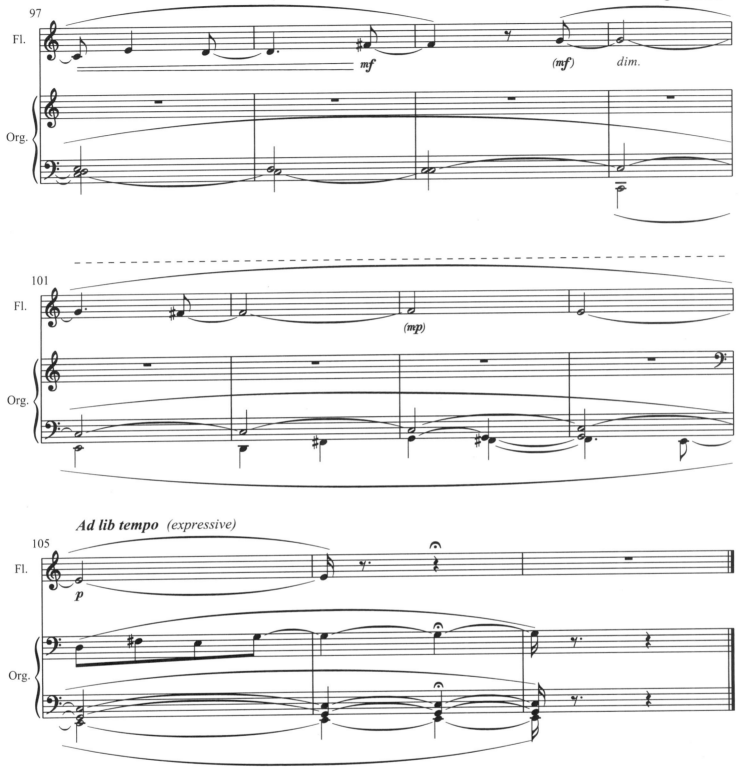

3. "Faith and Aspiration"
(Chaconne)

Warm and gently moving ($\frac{1}{2}$ = ca. 46)

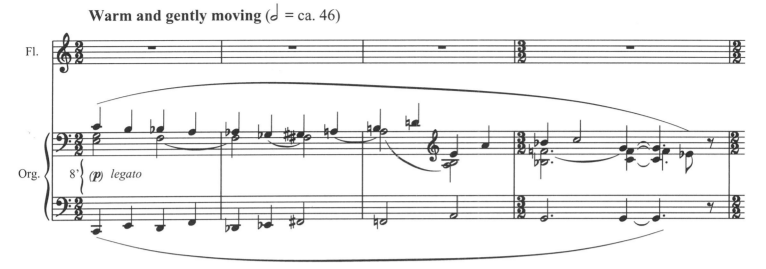

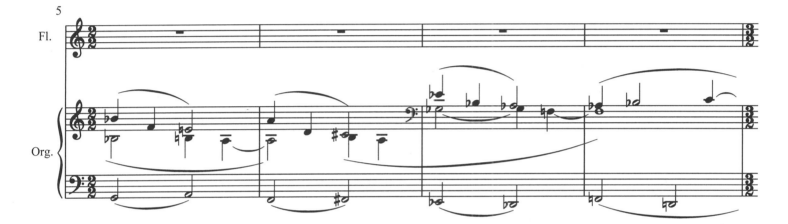

Expressive within ad lib tempo

Opening tempo

Expressive within ad lib tempo

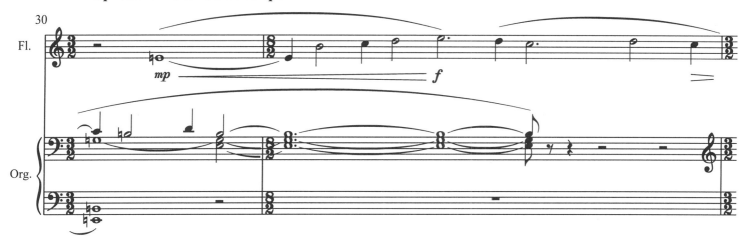

Opening tempo

Expressive within ad lib tempo

Opening tempo

Expressive within ad lib tempo

Start in opening tempo and move to Broader tempo

Slowing

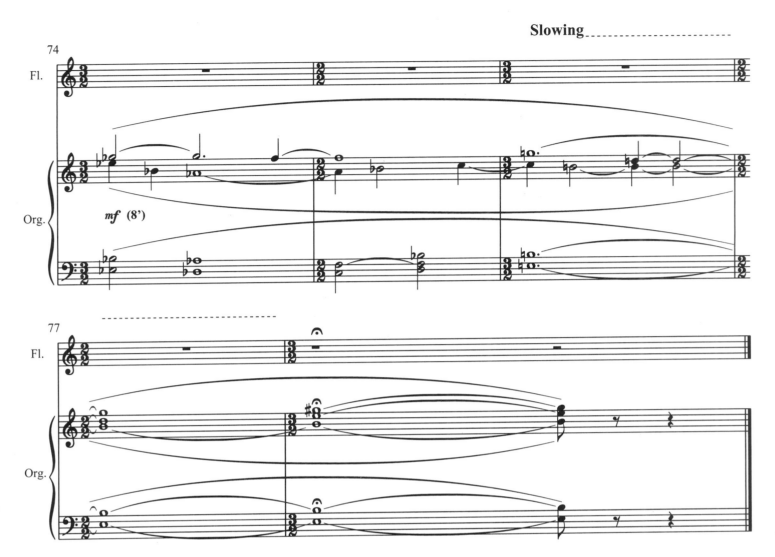

Fast and buoyant (♩ = ca.112)

*This entire movement may be played on 8',4', 2' stops.
Or, if desired, the organist may either observe the suggested
registrations or alternate more freely
between 8' 4' and 8' 4' 2' sonorities.

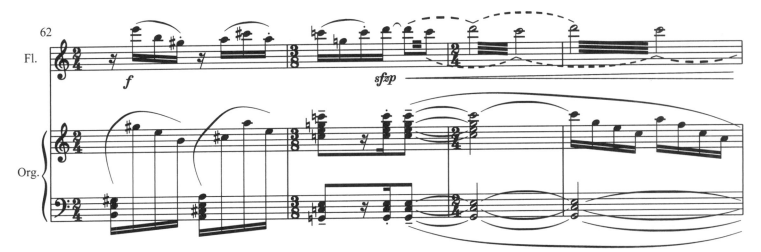

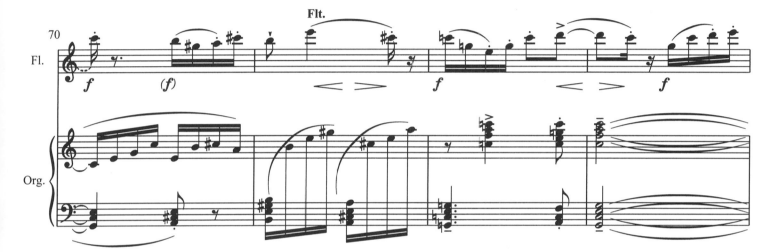

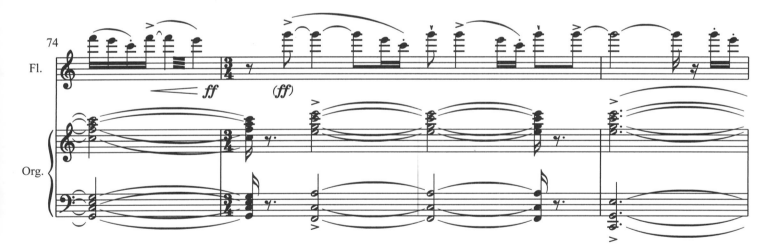

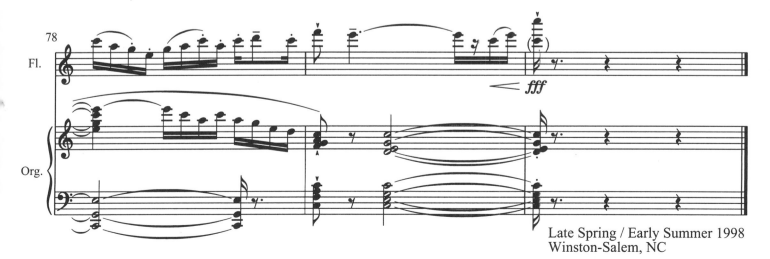

Late Spring / Early Summer 1998
Winston-Salem, NC